Singed Wings

Also by Lola Lemire Tostevin

Singed Wings

POEMS BY

LOLA LEMIRE TOSTEVIN

Talonbooks

Talonbooks

P.O. Box 2076, Vancouver, British Columbia, Canada V6B 3S3

www.talonbooks.com

Typeset in Adobe Jenson

Printed and bound in Canada on 100% post-consumer recycled paper

Typeset and cover design by Typesmith

First printing: 2013

The publisher gratefully acknowledges the financial support of the Canada Council for the Arts, the Government of Canada through the Canada Book Fund, and the Province of British Columbia through the British Columbia Arts Council and the Book Publishing Tax Credit for our publishing activities.

Library and Archives Canada Cataloguing in Publication

Tostevin, Lola Lemire, author
       Singed wings / Lola Lemire Tostevin.

ISBN 978-0-88922-790-3 (pbk.)

       I. Title.

PS8589.O6758S56 2013   C811'.54   C2013-904617-8

I play the role of a pudgy and
chatty little old lady.

— AGNÈS VARDA

CONTENTS

DAUGHTERS OF NECESSITY

Lit by its own light, each
Body is a place in itself

In spite of the edict: Do Not Touch
What is given to see is given to touch
As the eye becomes the sensing hand
Of her pellicular stone; her surfaces
Translucent as parchment
Tenuous as albumin skin of egg

Camille Claudel *statuaire*
Her birth to
          Presence

"You at least know what touches you,"
Rodin said, aware that of the five senses
Touch was the indispensable one
A matter of life or death

His eyes looking to hers to strip bare
To carve the knotted hands and feet
For his *Burghers of Calais*
Each stroke caught in his throat

His broad fingers excavate
The ridges of her spine
His flesh alive where hers began

How do you speak of what touches?
How do you dare write of it?

You could play, say, on touchstone
As in t)Ouch
When quick strokes of chisel
Hit too close to the bone

Touchline as a boundary
That should not be crossed

To be out of touch ...
Losing touch as a little insane
But not too much
Just a touch

How do you make sense
From an absence of sense
When the heart barely touches?

La Mer has nothing to do with the sea.
— CLAUDE DEBUSSY

Her body was incapable of abstraction
Each cell a place of refuge

Valéry could not take his eyes off her arms
Debussy loved everything she touched
The sea in which she bathed

They shared passions, Claude and Claudel
Turner. Poe. Music from Java
His studio a barcarole of water and light

Within this order of things
Everything conceived as sense
Made perfect sense

Until she returned to *Monsieur Rodin*

For twenty years, until his death, Debussy kept
Camille's *La Valse* on his piano, a woman's head

Nestled in the hollow of a man's clavicle
As on a missing pillow

Lovers keeping time
To eddies, ritornello waves

The lissom lines of lovers defying
The pull of empty space, his arm fastened
To her waist to maintain equilibrium

La Mer washing over
Lovers
Trapped inside an onyx
              Hokusai wave

Letters and photographs locked behind glass
Are as intrusive as the story of her life

If you know her story you will hear the panic
Rustle of her mother's black skirts upon learning
Her daughter's liaison with the infamous Monsieur

Her daughter's body soft and malleable
Surrenders to *la belle époque*

Subjected to its own ideals and ordering
The family intervenes to restore its own condition
Maintains its forms and norms

The language of unseeing dreams

On Quai Bourbon she rails against sleep
That threatens to seal her eyes
Her belly grown fat with conspiracy

She rails against art, part of the betrayal
Her studio floor scattered
      A hand
              here
A foot
      there

Torsos everywhere
Each one an aborted version of

Those who survive stand draped in white
Protected against light

The blind spot of those blinded by love
Ghosts of a former life

Because of a body of work
Placed under the sign of the body
Camille Claudel created a world
That held no place for her

She did not belong anywhere, yet
She would not have lived anywhere else

If you know her story, you will hear piety
Murmur in the frigid cells of the asylum
Nuns' eyes cast downward
Fingers caress worn wooden beads

She carves like a man, they whisper
Imagine her hands drifting along
Polished thighs of marble sentinels
Who rival devoted thoughts and nights
Ingestion of the body of Christ

She carves like a man, they whisper
Her sex and art twin slights that stifle souls
Cosseted inside long woollen robes
Crucifixes swaying from their hips

The nuns also knew the body intimately
Mainly to subtract from it

Du rêve que fut ma vie, ceci est le cauchemar.

— CAMILLE CLAUDEL
in a letter from the asylum

In an early photograph taken in the days
Of *Vertumne et Pomone,* those perfect angles
And planes only lovers can impersonate
She is defiant, proud, and indomitable

In the last known photograph she sits resigned
Toothless mouth
              Moth-
Eaten coat
Prey to other hands and eyes

This is what has become of *Pomone*
This is what has become of *The Wounded Niobid*

Camille Claudel's only failing
Was never carving a change of heart

Against days without lines or light
Nights that yield only blind stone
She dreamt

She dreamt of warmer coats
She dreamt of sweet butter
She dreamt of coffee from Brazil
She dreamt of *cerises à l'eau-de-vie*
She dreamt of tangerines
She dreamt of her childhood house

She dreamt of wings that would lift her
Beyond asylum walls

Wings so laden with dreams
No night was ever long enough

Each year her shadow grows smaller

Her voice finds only silence
Her throat a grave

Her hands alone in their touching

Locked up for thirty years
Makes as much sense as a sense lost
A touch-me-not

Camille Claudel
            Unborn

L'image se dissout
L'image du corps se dissout
Il ne reste que le vieux corps de l'anatomie
                              De la biologie

Corps qui s'excise de tous ses sens
Continue pourtant à articuler son espace

Why did it take so long to occupy her space
Sculptures as forsaken as her unmarked grave
Monument lost to lichen

"Genius is a mirror," she said
See
        Touch
              Hear with your eyes

The more you see her story, the less you hear
The split between soul and body

Where there is no coming to self
Without this otherness

> Clotho is the Daughter of Necessity.
>
> — PLATO

In a corner *Torse de Clotho*. Oh!
Scraps hanging to the skeleton within

Unlike the close proximity of lovers waltzing
Clotho stands by herself naked as a chicken neck
Nerve ends pulling at their roots

Old Clotho does not conform to some ideal
No. Hers is the body of exclusion
Visceral fatigue

Her vacant gaze brings truth to light
Then draws a flame over both eyes

The pseudonym kept silent for so long
Expresses the silence so long kept

Old Woman

No longer framed by that highest form of art
Clotho takes on Fate's features as she sails
Past Greek antiquity, even Willendorf

Faint memories
A lover's shoulder
Left oh, so hollow

Still, old Clotho insists on being seen
Rethinks herself
Creates new alphabets

A different birth
                To presence

I stand before Clotho and ache
With the history within

Like a missing shoulder, I ache
With the context I miss
The pain of a discarded limb

Old Woman, you are my guardian now
Let the damn body hang
Let it protect me from illusion

Old Woman

I am my own intruder.

Art is a Guarantee of Sanity.

— LOUISE BOURGEOIS

Unlike Claudel's asylum where memory slept
Bourgeois's *Cells* are where memory is transformed

"The past, too many people die of it,"
She says of *Vertumne et Pomone* overlooking
The garden of her childhood home at Choisy

The miniature replica of the pink house
Susceptible as newborn skin
Its entrance threatened by a guillotine

Bourgeois doesn't recreate the way she lived
She lives the way she recreates

There is an intimate relationship between women
And the houses in which they grew up
Spaces of happiness and unhappiness

Vintage chairs
One armchair an ample lap
Splintered mirrors that distort
Rickety beds and mattresses bearing
Marks of intimacy, pleasure, pain

Hands moved by love and fear

A small white dress hangs
Inside a flasher's trench coat

Two little blue rubber hearts
On a hook under the stairs

She hollows from the inside out

Glass vessels metaphors for the unstable
Body when emotion brews
Vats of precious liquids

Tears
Sweat
Blood
Semen
Vomit
Urine
Shit
Milk

A succession of breasts
Pink and velvety
Blind Man's Bluff

Downy penises I want to touch
When the guard isn't looking

Sucking cups
Shalimar flasks
Chanel dresses
Nylon stockings
Silk bloomers
Slips

Find their way back as
Objets d'art

In the museum gift shop a Mapplethorpe
Of Bourgeois wearing black monkey fur
Cradles an oversized phallus under one arm
The cunning smile of *Fillette*

Each *Cell* shares its secret

What to remember
What to forget
What to choose for its own understanding

Headless woman stretched out on
A bed – or a dinner table – inscribed
Je t'aime
Je t'aime
Je t'aime

At a dinner party femme fatale
Gets uncontrollable urges to sublimate

Cast pink-ochre lamb chops
In white plaster and serve them
To her guests for dinner

The split surface of crème brûlée
A gluey eye with a genital wink

Cross-stitched heads stand in a row

There is little difference between *Femme Maison*
Darning socks or mending Aubusson tapestries
Both are pleas for a second chance

Greenish blue skeins the colour of landscape
Purplish red from little female cochineals
Black the fast colour of sheep

The threaded needle is placed
At the periphery of what is missing
Moves back and forth in waves
Endless gestures of
                love
                    love
                        love

Winding, tightening

Cells as dynamic as honeycombs
Translucent as moon moths
Gathering sun
                wind
                      rain
Adjust to new morphologies
                        And more rain

Weighed down face
Puckered lips rubbery-soft gapes

All those useless hanging things

A Fashion Show of Body Parts
Contrives to speak what it once
Dared not think

"I do, I undo, I redo"

Endless loop of mending
Without a knot at the end of the thread

Spider on her dainty pointed feet
And articulated legs engineered for speed
Holds fast
                    La tricoteuse

Weaves her ambivalence
Between love and invasion

Between *Pregnant Woman*
And *Runaway Girl.*

> [The language of some writers] … moved me so
> powerfully that it moved into the drawings.
> I came to understand how I could combine the two.
>
> — BETTY GOODWIN

I take Goodwin at her word

An empty bed holds dreams of former sleepers
A flickering light bulb dim as pulse

Low-slung bedspring frayed from
Pushing, pushing, pushing
Until the pushing pulled

Figures without features or names
Falling
      Felled

Nest Six, graphite on wove paper
Draws its empty space where bird
Returns to start all over again

Memory follows inflections
From the sharp point of a stylus

Soft-ground shadings of *frottage*
Made by pressures of the hand

Double palms of labourers' gloves

Clothes lost to trunks and vintage stores
Retrieved as prisoners of war
A girl's sailor dress

Vests hold the past close to the chest
In shades of black-and-white photographs
Stashed away in taped-up boxes

Mute tumult of the heart
Being pushed through the press

Small kid glove, one of a pair, lacerated
By weather and time carries traces
Relic-like

Thrown as a challenge? A dual
Fought with miniature *épées*

Thin-boned wrist held out
For an eaglet's landing?

Maiden assize when the verdict
Carries no death sentence for a change

Pinked at the cuff with knotted silk strings
An alphabet to send furtive messages

A child walks hand in hand
With her father to a convent door
Notre-Dame-de-Lourdes

Not all senses grow senseless

In long, narrow corridors
The eye squints to better focus
A landscape of handprints

The head tilts left to move
The ear closer to the heart
Better to hear murmurings

Red passage
Colour of shame
Colour of blame

The odour of frailty clings
To hot-water bottles
Stale perfume

The altered gait of beaded slippers

Time always leaves signs
Where it has been

Why is that megaphone protruding
From an abdomen?
Or is it a back?

Better to hear the voice that speaks
Differently of different things

Thick as oil slick
Brittle as bone
Years rebuild themselves

Brackets
Steel rods and pulleys
Gears and switches
Fabric and thread
Plaster
Wire

Hold it all together

Waterproof sheets of Geofilm
Impersonate thin permeable skin

Make untouchable tangible

She folds, unfolds, refolds

Outsized tarpaulins scarred
By weather, sunlight, rain
Thick coats of gesso
Applied with strokes and slaps

Old tarp halves stacked in corners
Find their way together again
Like golden anniversary couples

Imitate fingered spines on library shelves
Romance
        Horror
Wind around each other
Double helices of replication

The paradox of lives held
Between
        Hier-
Aujourd'hui

Swimmer bobs barely above
Seeks a helping hand from the elemental
Where there is no catch of breath

Reflected light offers little perspective
Other than the surface it illuminates

When face to face with nakedness
Hands and eyes chart their paths
To mine

Swimmer
Femme Maison
Clotho

Words and Works by whom
I might be otherwise.

XIV PHILIPPICS

After Cicero

Reversals are at hand

Banished by the years, her womanliness
Deserts her as she bemoans the ingratitude
Wreck of her ambitions

A feminist in her prime, her poems bore
Testimony to this skill. Some wit
Some eloquence. So

Shouldn't age now ease the weight
That wrings the heart? Shouldn't the mind
Be better ordered and equable?

She rarely thought of age
A fable perhaps
One that lacked conviction

That was then

Are the years less disagreeable now
Than they will be, say, in her ninetieth?

How did age steal womanhood faster
Than womanhood stole childhood?

The usual charges:
Old age lacks sensual pleasures

Sex. Everywhere sex
So that when everything is named "sex"
Nothing is named

Neglected by those from whom she once received
Attentions, it seems the blame is laid on the wrong thing
Only fools impute their frailties and their guilt

Old women who are neither cross-grained
Nor churlish find old age tolerable enough

Often look at old men and conclude that
Not hankering is perhaps the gentler thing ·

Advice to the lovelorn: Remember
What Sophocles said when asked
If he were still a lover. "Heaven forbid!
I was only too happy to escape from that boorish master
It cannot be named lack who does not desire"

How many bushels of apples is she expected to eat
Naked and wrinkled by the old gnarled tree?

How many wilted oak leaves
Is she expected to iron?

Listen. The nibbled apples have all been gathered
The cicadas stuck in their long drones have starved

Remember: Desire only survives
In future perfect

Seldom beyond *La petite mort*

Cicero had many sayings

While the crew is busy climbing
Others hurry down
Others pump out bilge water
Old Woman sits quietly in the stern
And holds the tiller

Yeah ... That saying

Hannah Arendt said it better:
"Loneliness is more apt to show itself
In the noisy company of others

Wen de cheeps are down
You must make some choices"

Or when a notorious writer / womanizer
Made a pass, she gently placed her hand
On his: "Let me be zee exception"

When they say age withdraws
From active employment, do they mean
Employment carried by bodily strength?

She no more misses it than a young woman
Misses the strength of a mule or a cow

At no time was she known for her biceps
And time was brief when she was known for her breasts

Best to tell what she can now
Since time will soon disallow
The silence that is required

The body withdraws
To rethink itself

The spotted and wrinkled skin
Slips like a glove onto the writing hand

Touches on the strangeness
Of this otherness

Unless you believe in literalist dogma
There is no resolution
As one reader suggests

No accurate calculations as Einstein's
Who whispered on his deathbed
"If only I'd had more mathematics"

No. She won't be caught lamenting
"If only I'd had more poems"

Words come and go
Give and take
Tell tall tales and sometimes truth

The truth of the matter is truth
Has little to say for itself

Always on the move
Tectonic

Words hold on as if they were hands
Spread themselves in wild profusion

It's like Cicero said: "Those who use them
Will play the drama to its end"

It's like Cicero said:
"Life occurs at different ages
While words occur at all stages"

Travel from beginning to end
From passion to indifference
Then all the way back again

Agnès Varda walks her camera
Among purple-coloured cabbages
Collects heart-shaped potatoes
Leaves them on a shelf to rot

Oui, je vieillis, she says on her eightieth birthday
Staring at a clock with no hands
Voice-overs paired with images of herself

"And why shouldn't I implicate myself in my films?
Have I no place in my own writing?"

Stares into the camera: "What does it mean
To be ahead of your time?"

No greater misery than to be told
That the young deride the old

When, at a reading, she tells a young poet
He has beautiful eyes
He and his friend snicker

Youth is a prism through which young men
(And old men who think themselves young)
Like to catch a glimpse of themselves unaware
It is precisely through this prism that old women
Will catch them at their own narcissism

Hold their eyes within their gaze

So. To all the young poets with beautiful eyes
Let me tell you how the years will metastasize

You too will be confronted with desire
When the would-be lover
Is no other than the absent reader

Days still when she imagines herself the dignified
Old broad sipping a *café crème* in a Haussmann
Building reading *À la recherche du temps perdu*
A twelve-tone piano composition in the background

Other days when she yearns for one more scandal
No, not a love affair ... well ... A glass of Chardonnay
While rereading the bath scene in *L'homme flambé*

So. To the French academic who disapproved
Of a glass of wine too many at some literary event
Va te faire foutre, vieille chichiteuse

Wine and insult replenish so much better
Than literary events ever can

Like good old Dorothy Livesay said
Standing in line at Union Station
When a young man in railway uniform
Tells her, "C'mon, move it up, granny"
Livesay answers, "Fuck you, sonny"

Each morning she quibbles a little with Descartes
The thinking thing
The body thing

It lacks nuance

Descartes probably didn't even know
How to laugh. There's little humour in a mental
Encounter that fails to feature any of the senses

Each morning when limb by limb
She unravels out of bed
And like any old Lear scratching his bony ass
She begins the day by emptying her bladder

Puts on the non-voice of Leonard Cohen
Backed by strings and a choir: "For he's touched
Your perfect body with his mind"

Makes coffee
Reflects how easily thinking follows
The crucial actions assigned to being

She feels nothing from the waist down
Acutely aware of the short hospital gown
While the doctor lifts her legs to measure
The discrepancy caused by too many years

Every few seconds she places her hand over
Her scrubby pubic area. Every few seconds
The doctor tells his attendants to remove her hand
Until they pin both down

She is vaguely aware of the sound of tapping
Thin end of a hammer against stone
The unwavering certainty of the bone breaker

She writes, unwrites, rewrites

Cooks lamb chops for dinner
Takes grandkids to the park
A woman full of hours
A woman full of days

Between the quiet limits of words
There is shouting and scuffling
Fearless twists and turns on monkey bars

Sanctuary of the sandbox
With its simple geometric forms

Persistent requests for
Rock, Paper, Scissors
Triumphing over the other
Rock overcome by paper

One grandmother on a swing
Pumps her varicose legs and soars
Her flowered dress balloons and curves
Free will restored by free won't

The place from which the fear of failing
Is transformed into the art of knowing how to fail

PUNCTUM

I like certain biographical features which, in a writer's life, delight me as much as certain photographs; I have called these features "biographemes": Photography has the same relation to History that the biographeme has to biography.

A photograph of a child facing a body of water
Takes her to some other place
                              Some other time.

It could be any child in baggy shorts past his knees
Oversized sweatshirt, hands camouflaged
By long sleeves.

Blond curls under a canvas hat scrunched
Over his ears.

The more she gazes at the photograph
The more it divides itself in two: a child
Observing a bay on Lake Huron: a child
Being observed.

The studium is of the order of liking, not of loving …

… occasionally (but alas all too rarely) a "detail" attracts me. I feel that its mere presence changes my reading, that I am looking at a new photograph, marked in my eyes with a higher value. "This detail" is the punctum.

A circle on his back, trademark
Of a sportswear company
Resembles a target.
                    Centre of gravity shoots
An arrow into her eyes.
Implants itself. Waits.

                    For the right moment
                    To claim its presence.

Punctuates the heart.
Midpoint of a lonely circle.

She retrieves a shoebox held together
With tape.
                    Riffles through
For a photograph of herself
Standing on a shore.

The lake is small and shallow.
                    An illusion when distance
                    Reduces all points
Along its horizon.

She is facing the photographer.
Her blond hair is artificially curled.
Her mother's Kodak Brownie
Rewinding.

The photographs remind her of a recent exhibition.
The historical development of melancholia
From antiquity to Dürer's *Knight and Death*
To the harsh light of digital images.

Monk by the Sea by Caspar David Friedrich
Is central to the exhibition.

Back to the viewer, a lone figure at the edge
Of a windswept sea merged with flinty sky
Conveys the immensity of what lies
Before him.

Except Friedrich did not capitulate:

Moonrise
The Wanderer above the Sea of Fog
The Stages of Life
Generations
Woman at Dawn
Sunset

Blank mirrors where gulls flutter and screech
Sharpen their beaks on early-morning air.
                              Cross boundaries between
Formlessness and form
Beyond a geography of limits.

There are no gulls in either photograph
As when hand in hand, they walk through wild
Grass
                    Thick as pampas blades
                    Dank with dew. Through

Flowering nettle merged with
Sky the colour of underdisks of wild
Rose leaves when clouds begin to moult
Before the sun.

Somewhere an abacus woodpecker counts
Rings in trunks of trees.

                    Her grandson's eyes brown rushes
                    Reflect for the first time

This ancient world.

Lured by its shelter, she travels through
Black rock where land opens up
On Providence Bay.
                              Nest of moss,
Stone, pine needles, abandoned shells
Where life turns on itself.

Time begins
                    Time ends
                                        Time begins again

She follows yellow lady slippers that run
By the side of the road from Little Current
To South Baymouth where evening sinks
Below the horizon
                              A giant discus fish.

Loon's cry from Lake Manitou. Timeless
Heartache. Hieroglyphs of geese tracks.
Gentle breeze vocable of breath
That begins with a sigh then disappears
                              Into the great hollow.

There is no temporal dimension to this island
Where memories are as old as Confucian Odes.

Waves curdle and gurgle in his tiny
Footsteps.

        Pockets full of shells and tiny crabs
        Hair sporting half a dozen kittiwake quills.

Head filled with questions
Time will soon wear down smooth
        As the skeletal remains of a bird he found.

His hand in hers an assemblage of bird bones.
Translucent, brittle as the needle-billed
Skull.

Ultimately, Photography is subversive not when it frightens,
repels, or even stigmatizes, but when it is pensive, when it thinks.

The photograph cannot convey what she feels
Other than tenderness and fear. And the one
Word tucked inside the loop of its one syllable.

In this, language too turns
Its back.

      No longer a name-giving grasp
      To capture the one elusive word.

Little hermit curled within
The mystery of his encounters.

      Hawk circles on veering wings
      The silk shroud of a wasp's nest.

And she knows.
A child who enters this place
Will grow to imagine submerged under water
The most arid of deserts.

When far from the immensity of Lake Huron.
The intimacy of Manitoulin Island.

When city sky presses down heavy
As whetstone, she returns to the photograph.

Small figure lost in details
Of light and shade.

              Raw materials that make a lifetime
                Of each and every moment. Perceive

Intimate and secret relations of things.

This island grown old and worn
Is a new island too.

Her grandson amplifies the sky.
Takes her to perspectives filled with clarity.

A space of elsewhere without bounds
Old word this world of new *love*.

SINGED WINGS

Mais elle ne peut pas ne pas écrire

Il lui faut des histoires
Histoires d'amour
Histoires de meurtres
Histoires banales

Elle ne peut rien lâcher
Ni la table
Ni les mots qui arrivent sur la page

Rien ne peut exister que cela

Il lui faut aussi des poèmes

Sinon, c'est à mourir
Dit-elle

No accident part of the brain
Stores the years as semantic memory

If not for words, how would years survive

Thrive on borrowed time
Each bead gliding upon axon

                Until one goes off circuit
                Begins new connections

Common tricks of distortion
Or the reductionist approach

Revisits old stories when love
Could only love one at a time

When practice almost never made perfect

The heart resets each morning and night
According to the earth's rotations
Orbits at relative velocities
                    Heavy in winter
                    Lighthearted in summer

As when she looked to a small lake
In Northern Ontario to measure
The depth of her existence

Until depth no longer needed measuring

The child at the edge of a riverbed
Has crossed the line

The erratic heart is nothing more
Or less
Than the site from which
It appeared young
                    Then old into the world

It is mere existence
Mere content

A night science at best
Between not quite and not yet
She dreams in French

Le poème s'instaure par divers moyens
Son espace et son temps ne coïncident
Pas toujours avec le quotidien

Selon sa mise en perspective sa vie continue
Comme avant
                                Elle voyage à bord d'un train
Où le temps ne change jamais du début
Jusqu'à la fin

Resin, the sharp taste of terpene
When pinesap rolled into balls
Is chewed like gum

Gives evergreens their touch of colour
An interior turned inside out

Gives forest a full dimension
Among the warblers

Claims its existence

Before amber blood lines
Turn into death traps
For wasps, bees, and ants

Each year extends the range
Of her inventions

Recalibrates what is old into something
New. A contradiction in terms

Now that youth and sex appeal
No longer draw attention, she relies on wit
Platonic friendships, kindness, malice
Happiness

The ransom of formalism
Is the permission to love and live
Still

> My work is surely connected to me,
> but I cannot judge it, nor do I need to.
>
> — PINA BAUSCH

We have all sat at Café Müller
Mindful of the artful way we hold a cigarette
Gestures carved in smoke
                    Billie Holiday in the background

We have all taken poses
Seductive tangos in basic black
                    Pearl earrings

Dark striped suits moving along
An axis of passion and aggression

Changed partners on cue
Started over the insatiable geometries

His hand around her waist
Her head on his shoulder

The rituals behind which
                    We all disappear

Like the old sock that needs mending
The poem concentrates on absence

A six-year-old makes her way through
Winter's whiplash, snow swirling around her
A gang of guardian angels

Her loosened braid caught in this northern light

Red sumac peers against shale
Pitted by weather and mining

Frail saplings doggedly take root
Nettles flower along the edge of ruin

Human landscapes too

Giacometti figures blackened and gouged
Long feet lumpish
Torsos knuckled forward

Small heads ravaged by snow and soot

Ongoing meditations across rock
Through treetops

        Perfect geometries of geese along
        Parallel bands of land and sky

House by a lake threatened by weather
Trees that twist and turn as if possessed

Worn images unaware
They have been written before

What is repeated is not what they mean
But what they no longer mean

        Each image a stepping stone for portaging
        What can't be held or meant

As when white-throated sparrows
Take flight in the form of a bare tree
And suddenly fly through her

LICHENS

A Symbiotic Association

Cambrian Shield, worn spine, worn icon
Ragged conifers stripped

        Of their cosmic implications
        Barely hold on

Smaller kettles of hawks

Strolls on Cup and Saucer Trail

        Require walking sticks
        Flippers for Lac des Pins

Algues
    vagues
        Echolalia of what's left
Of mother tongue
        Langue outre-mère

From her study in Toronto a confused hum
Of traffic, jackhammers, leaf blowers. Ongoing
Reverberation of meaningless noise

Banished from the realm of possibility
Her intimate space loses clarity
                    Cells and nerves besieged

Hands poised over her keyboard
She craves new anatomies and landscapes

                    While a sharp pain traces a trajectory
                    On either side of her spine. A radial burst

Along the spinal canal

There is an inherent impossibility to writing
Poetically about bodies and landscapes

What are needed are scientific facts and graphs
Fibrillating hearts heard through stethoscopes

Poetry is phenomenology without the phenomena
An undoing of orders as it follows different paths

From Cambrian Shield
Cup and Saucer Trail
Swim in Lac des Pins

When poetry dreams of landscape
It dreams in proportion

To the body that inhabits it

One doctor diagnoses the silver plaques
Spreading over her back as scleroderma
Thick skin

A second doctor believes the plaques are related
To sensitivities to the environment
Lichen planus

Named for its resemblance to silver flat-lace
That spreads over rock or hangs from trees
                              In thick filigree tapestries

She reads up on lichens

For 400 million years lichens have developed strategies
Of survival when two or more types of organisms
Live in permanent relationships

Choose barren and inhospitable terrains
Where they begin the slow process of creating
Foundations for habiting with other life forms

They can remain dormant indefinitely
Survive extreme cold

Eat stone

Landscapes are immeasurable unless they flow
Inside our veins
                    Breathe through our breath

We are the inhabitants of the forests of ourselves
We are nests that fall under our own weight

                    Fronds that unfurl into space

Each and every one is a universe
In every sense of the word

Science tells us when ferns
Reduced to ashes are dissolved
In pure water and the water evaporates

All that is left are crystals
In the form of a fern frond

When she is cremated
                    Her ashes dissolved in water

All that will be left will be crystals
In the form of lichens
From the woods of Northern Ontario
And the Laurentians

LA FIESTA DE LOS MUERTOS

Feet, why do I need them if I have wings.

— FRIDA KAHLO

Peg-leg Frida drinks tequila
Like a Jalisco mariachi
                    To drown her pain

Until the pain learns how to swim

Fills her canvas with local colour
                    Fœtus flowers
                    Sliced hearts

The steel rod holding her spine
Her coat of arms

This is life
The rest is painted bread

A body in pain carries its own clarity
A tinge of solitude

From the mirror fitted on the underside
Of her bed canopy she paints alter egos

Girl with Death Mask (She Plays Alone)
Pre-Columbian terracotta statuettes
A Few Little Pricks
Monkeys

She listens to the orange tree bear
Watermelon, pineapple, mangos

The tintinnabulation of rain on tiled roof
Followed by waves of stillness
The sound of solitude

Each morning when the slow lid lifts
La Casa Azul is made bluer by the glitter
Of bones from long lines of ancestors
And her amputated limb

The acanthus sits in eternal life
Next to the white-haired cactus
With the comb-over

A wobbly bat chases its shadow
Round and round the garden walls

The bellied bindweed threatens to go over

Yellow roses waver in prayer
Honeysuckle crawls on clawed knees

Flies peruse Granizo's morning pee
Little pet deer

After a long night's prowl
Cat naps by the cannas

Capulina, the itzcuintli dog, stretches
Before posing for her portrait

Each day is the same

Prosthetic leg
Wheelchair
Plaster corsets painted with condor wings
Easel
Brushes
Paints
A looking glass

Through which she paints
The most perfect image
Of her imperfect body

Each day is different

Destined for Noah's ark
Everyone at la Casa Azul is paired

The dogs Capiluna and Señor Xolotl
The monkeys Fulang-Chang and el Caimito
Two turkeys
Two doves
Hen and rooster
Fish
Diego and Frida
Her crocheted elbow-length gloves

Her legs were also once a pair
Until one ran off to become a nimble dancer

The one left behind alone and lame

She is held together by prosthesis
Sporting a red embroidered Chinese boot

She is held together by satin ribbons
Hair braided in a chaplet
Bougainvillea crown

She is held together by knotted fringe
Silk threads
Organdy
Pleated cotton lace
Double cloth sacks
So ancient they are lost to time

She is held together by a *rebozo* shawl
Thirty-three inches wide and two yards long
Which serves
As empty crib
Coat
Bandage
Hammock
Lap
Screen
Shroud

She is held together with silk
Reinforced with crêpe de Chine
Loom, spindle, weaving comb
Brocade

She is held together by Mayan jade
Aquamarine
Appliqué
Percale
Taffeta and flounce

She is held together by bone lace

> Her art is a ribbon around a bomb.
>
> — ANDRÉ BRETON

In America she never paints gringos
Their houses bread ovens
Their faces unbaked rolls

In Paris the couturiers want to copy Madame's
Tehuana skirts and ruffled petticoats

French surrealists claim her as their own
While la mestiza swears under her breath

Those sons of bitches with their waking dreams
What do they know
Of being speared by a streetcar rail
With two angels astride as on a seesaw

Each night la mestiza goes to bed
With seagull wings and fish fins

Never paints dreams
Never has to

Because plantain leaves folded
Into bowls remain empty

Because too many bellies
Grow hollow as gourds

La mestiza cuts her hair
Hybrid revolutionary
In boots, denim cap, and jacket

Half-woman
Half-man
Half-man
Half-condor
Half-condor
Half-child
Half-child
Half-tree
Half-tree
Half-artery
One
Half
Always
On
The
Look
Out

When the body turns on itself
When it comes to an understanding
That it is only the matter of time

It reinvents itself as metaphor

Imagines what the eye can barely see
Feels where the hands can barely reach

Family resemblances disappear

Pesky little beauty spots
Pop up everywhere
                    A new carnal topography

Areolas transform into cracked nipples
Lunules into brittle nails
Wet kiss a drool

The body reinvents itself as soul

The mirror from which she painted
Is replaced by a skeleton
Body without husk

La Casa Azul is where she was born
La Casa Azul is where she will die
Forty-three years stretched taut

From her self-portraits at the AGO
Frida Kahlo watches viewers
Watching her

Their point of view her point of view
Accomplices, each on a half-footing

What I take away are not self-portraits
Of la mestiza but a space
Where I am left standing

De plus en plus
Le poème exprime
Un passé composé

Il n'arrive pas à tout dire
Éprouve même la sensation
De n'avoir rien dit

S'amuse pourtant à déplacer
Ses lettres afin que le monde des singes
Devienne le monde des signes

ACKNOWLEDGEMENTS

For the last few years, I have explored the creativity of
women who practised their art either under unfavourable
social or physical circumstances, such as Camille Claudel
and Frida Kahlo, or into advanced age, such as Louise
Bourgeois and Betty Goodwin. I have travelled to several
cities to attend Pina Bausch's dance troupe and choreography
as I have for Marie Chouinard. I never miss a novel, a film, a
play, an interview, or biography featuring Marguerite Duras,
or a book by or a biography of Hannah Arendt, or the films
of Agnès Varda. My writing practice is modest compared to
these women's art yet they nudge me to keep on. With each
additional year, I grow more grateful.

The section on Camille Claudel was written after I attended
a retrospective at the Musée Rodin in Paris in 2008.

I have attended two retrospectives of Louise Bourgeois's
work at the Centre Pompidou and visited many of her works
in other museums, especially the extensive collection at the
Guggenheim Museum in Bilbao, Spain.

Most of the poems of the Betty Goodwin sequence are
based on the retrospective *The Art of Betty Goodwin* at the
Art Gallery of Ontario, November 1998 to March 1999,
and its accompanying catalogue.

The poems on Frida Kahlo were written following an
exhibition at the AGO in November 2012. On the day I
attended I received an email from Garry Thomas Morse, my
poet editor at Talonbooks, suggesting I write an additional
section to my manuscript. A few days later, I received an
unsolicited book, *Frida Kahlo: Painting Her Own Reality* from a

long-time friend, Carol Beaven. The coincidences were too palpable to ignore. I am deeply grateful to them.

My thanks to Talonbooks, especially Garry Thomas Morse for his fine editing, Greg Gibson for his patience, and Ann-Marie Metten for her production editing.

My gratitude to Jerry Tostevin and my daughter, Lisa.

"XIV Philippics" was inspired by Cicero's *Cato Major; or, a Treatise on Old Age*.

An early version of "Punctum" was published as a chapbook by Nomados Literary Publishers of Vancouver in 2007. It is dedicated to my grandchildren, Caleb, Ethan, and Quintin.

The Roland Barthes quotes are from *Camera Lucida: Reflections on Photography*, trans. Richard Howard. New York: Hill and Wang, 1983.

In "Punctum," the photograph of a child is by Peter Tostevin.

The photograph of the writer as a young girl is by Laurette Lemire.

An earlier version of "Lichens: A Symbiotic Relationship" appeared in *Ars Medica* 6 (2011): 21.

ABOUT THE AUTHOR

LOLA LEMIRE TOSTEVIN is a bilingual Canadian writer who writes mainly in English. She is the author of three novels, eight collections of poetry, numerous pieces of short fiction, and a collection of literary essays and criticism. She has translated into English the work of many writers, including Anne Hébert, Hector de Saint-Denys Garneau, Nicole Brossard, and Paule Thévenin, and she has translated into French Michael Ondaatje's *Elimination Dance*. Her novel *Frog Moon* was translated into French and two of her collections of poetry, *Color of Her Speech* and *'sophie*, were translated into Italian. Her most recent novel, *The Other Sister*, was published in the fall of 2008.

Tostevin has taught creative writing at York University, Toronto, and served as writer-in-residence at the University of Western Ontario, London. She is presently preparing a second collection of literary essays and is working on a series of short fictions.